Auditory Memory Games for Kids

WH-Questions

Recalling

Short Stories

Welcome to Auditory Memory Game for Kids: Recalling, Wh- Questions and Short Stories. This workbook is filled with exercises that help children develop auditory memory for details they listen to.

If you are looking for a comprehensive workbook that contains different auditory memory for wh-questions, auditory memory for short stories, or want to reproduce auditory memory cards for your children or students, the set of items in this material is exactly what you need.

Auditory memory is such an important skill to handle conversations, academic tasks, or other daily life tasks. By having a specific workbook catered to help in auditory memory for quick stories, questions, and details, you can sharpen this skill in your children or students.

Read each item to the child orally and ask them to recall the items. You may provide prompts by saying the items again or giving clues depending on the child's skill level.

Shopping

Lena went to the grocery store on Monday. She shopped for milk and bread. What did she shop for?

Alice went to the toy store to buy some gifts for her baby sister. She bought a teddy bear and a ball. What did she buy?

My aunt went to the mall this morning. She shopped for a pair of pink shoes and blue boots. What did she shop for?

Shopping

Mr. Smith went to the supermarket yesterday. He shopped for cereals and canned goods. What did he shop for?

Emma went to a boutique to try out some new clothes. She chose a skirt and a yellow dress. What did she buy?

David went to a neighbor's garage sale. He chose a vase and some garden tools. What did he buy?

Ordering in a Restaurant

Jacob ordered in the restaurant. He asked for fries, chocolate ice cream, and a burger. What did he order?

Simon likes Italian food. He asked for a whole pizza, a plate of spaghetti, and Tiramisu. What did he order?

My parents had a dinner date on their anniversary. They asked for a bottle of wine, steak, and salad. What did they order?

Ordering in a Restaurant

John, Sally and Mary had snacks in a small cafe. They had cupcakes, fruit shakes, and sandwiches. What did they order?

Henry likes Japanese food. He always asks for a hot bowl of ramen with meat, egg, and vegetables. What is in Henry's bowl of ramen?

Mr. Brown stopped by a diner after a long drive. He asked for grilled chicken, garlic bread, and coffee. What did he order?

Travelling

Gail rode the car. She saw a bird, bushes, a stop sign, and a dog outside. What did she see?

Karen traveled by airplane with her parents. She saw through the plane window the blue sky, some large clouds, wide landcapes, and the ocean, What did she see?

Johnny went on a cruise holiday with his uncle. He saw big waves in the sea, some sailboats, dolphins jumping, and seagulls flying. What did he see?

Traveling

Mrs. Davis travelled the countryside by train. She saw hills, a herd of cattle, a bridge, and a river. What did she see?

Joe and Jenny went biking at the park. They saw people, benches, trees, and grass. What did they see?

Emma rode a bus to school. She saw some children, houses, shops, and cars. What did she see?

Read each item orally and ask the child corresponding wh- questions. Repeat the item or provide prompts and cues as needed.

**Hickory dickory dock,
the mouse ran up the clock,
the clock struck one,
the mouse ran down,
hickory dickory dock.**

Questions:

Who ran up the clock?

What happened when the clock struck one?

**Humpty Dumpty sat on a wall
Humpty Dumpty had a great fall
All the king's horses
and all the king's men
Couldn't put Humpty
together again.**

Questions:

Who sat on a wall?

**What happened when Humpty
Dumpty fell?**

Jack and Jill went up the hill
To fetch a pail of water.
Jack fell down and broke his crown,
And Jill came tumbling after.

Questions:

Who went up the hill?

What happened when Jack fell down?

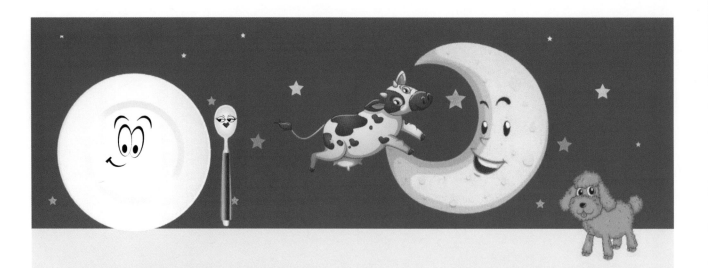

Hey, diddle, diddle, the cat and the fiddle
The cow jumped over the moon
The little dog laughed to see such fun
And the dish ran away with the spoon.

Questions:

Who jumped over the moon?

What happened when it jumped over the moon?

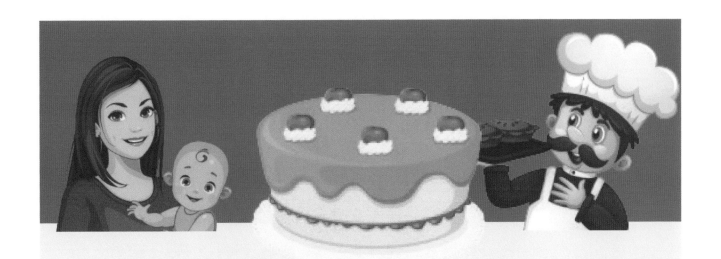

Pat-a-cake, pat-a-cake baker's man
Bake me a cake as fast as you can
Pat it and prick it and mark it with "B"
Put it in the oven for baby and me.

Questions:

Who will bake me a cake?

What will the baker's man do with the cake?

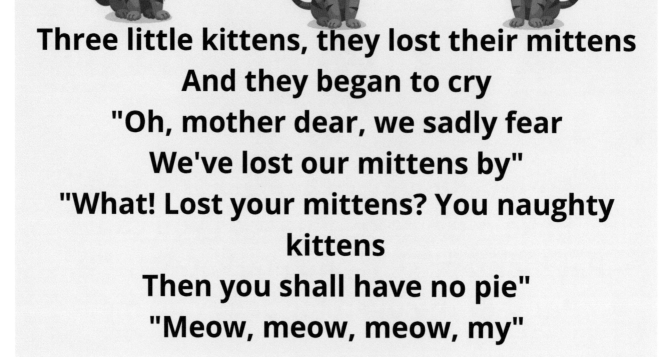

Three little kittens, they lost their mittens
And they began to cry
"Oh, mother dear, we sadly fear
We've lost our mittens by"
"What! Lost your mittens? You naughty kittens
Then you shall have no pie"
"Meow, meow, meow, my"

Questions:

Who lost their mittens?

What happened when they lost their mittens?

Birthday Party Invitations

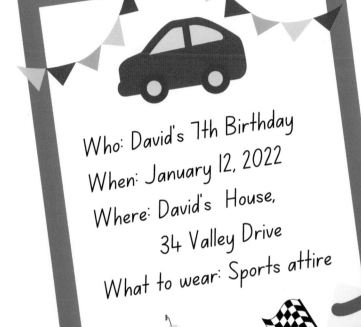

Who: David's 7th Birthday
When: January 12, 2022
Where: David's House,
34 Valley Drive
What to wear: Sports attire

Read the items on each birthday invitations and ask the child the corresponding wh-questions.

Who: Martin's 4th Birthday
When: August 15, 2022
Where: Newport Beach
What to wear: Nautical outfit

Birthday Party Invitations

Who: Angelo's Birthday
When: May 3, 2022
Where: At the Community Center
What to wear: A funny hat

Who: Ashley's 2nd Birthday
When: September 15, 2022
Where: Smith Residence
What to bring: Swimming attire
                and towels

Birthday Party Invitations

PAJAMA PARTY

Who: Meghan's 5th Birthday
When: April 10 from 4pm-8pm
Where: Jones Residence
What to wear: Your favorite
pajamas!

PAR-TEA

Who: Stella's 8th Birthday
When: Saturday, July 10 4:30 pm
Where: Lakewood Gardens
What to wear: Fanciest attire

Read each story to the child orally and ask the following wh- questions. You may repeat the story or provide cues and prompts depending on the child's skill.

Baking A Rainbow Cake

Martha and her mom are going to bake a rainbow cake. They needed flour, eggs, vanilla extract, sugar, butter and milk. They mixed all the ingredients together and baked it in the oven for 25 minutes. The cake smelled so good! They put a white frosting on top with rainbow sprinkles. Martha said it was the best rainbow cake ever.

1. What did Martha and her mom bake?
2. Give 3 ingredients they used for the cake.
3. How many minutes did they bake the cake in the oven?

A Cat is Rescued

Owen's cat loves chasing squirrels. But one day, the cat went too far chasing a squirrel! Owen's cat got stuck in a tree branch and could not come down. Thankfully, the tree was near the fire station. They asked a fireman to help set a ladder to bring Owen's cat down. Thanks to the fireman, now Owen's cat is safe.

1. Who owns a cat?
2. What does Owen's cat love to chase?
3. What did the fireman use to bring the cat down from the tree?

Snack Time in School

Ring! The bell rang at 10:00 in the morning and it is snack time in Julie's school. Julie sat with her friends, Ben and Ella. Julie opened her lunch box and she had a ham and cheese sandwich. Ben had some fresh chocolate chip cookies. Ella had a yummy apple with caramel sauce. Everyone decided to share their snack with each other. They had a great time.

1. When is Julie's snack time in school?
2. Who are Julie's friends?
3. What was Ella's snack?

Going to the Beach

Tonya is excited because her family is going to the beach. Her mom said, "Don't forget to bring your sunglasses and beach toys!". She remembered to pack those things in her blue backpack. When they arrived at the beach, Tonya put sunblock on her face, arms and legs. The view was so beautiful with the blue skies, white sand, and the blue ocean! They saw some sailboats from far away while Tonya was playing with her beach toys in the sand.

1. What did Tonya's mom tell her to bring?
2. What was the first thing Tonya did when they arrived at the beach?
3. What did they see at the beach from afar?

A Visit to the Dentist

Lucas is scheduled to visit the dentist. His dad drove him to Dr. Wilson's dental office. Lucas is a little scared at first, but when he entered the room, the dental hygienist was friendly. She cleaned Lucas' teeth and Dr. Wilson arrived to show X-rays and checked his mouth. "Great! You have no cavities!" Dr. Wilson said. Lucas was relieved and he got a goody bag from Dr. Wilson.

1. Who is Lucas' dentist?
2. What did Lucas feel about going to the clinic?
3. What did Dr. Wilson say when she checked Lucas' mouth?

Thank You!

Found this book helpful? Don't forget
to give us a 5-Star Review. It helps us
create more useful workbooks like these.
It also helps our small business thrive.
We appreciate it so much!

Printed in Great Britain
by Amazon

24998619R00018